Simply The Best

A collection of persuasive letters fr

by Tony Norman

Contents

Section 1
Best Place to Live: **Eastbourne**   2
Best Sports Star: **David Beckham**   8

Section 2
Best Holiday: **Orlando Theme Parks**   12
Best Pop Band: **The Beatles**   16

Section 3
Best Artist: **Vincent van Gogh**   22
Best Way to Travel: **Steam Trains**   28

A Final Letter from the Author   32

Edinburgh Gate
Harlow, Essex

Best Place to Live: Eastbourne

Dear Readers,

Eastbourne is simply the best place to live in the whole world. It's my home town and I love it – so that makes me the best person to tell you how good it is.

Let me tell you about my town …

Eastbourne is a seaside resort on the south coast of England. It's a top spot for holidays. Visitors might have to sit in their cars for hours to get there. But local people can go for a swim any time they like.

When you live in Eastbourne, every day is like a holiday. Can you say the same about your town?

Sun over the sea at Eastbourne

I never get bored in Eastbourne because there is so much to do. We have great shops, theatres, cinemas and places to eat. You can walk along the pier, or fish from the beach. You can go ten-pin bowling or go-karting and there is even a mini railway to ride on.

The South Downs are above the town. Here you'll find green hills and fields, where sheep graze and llamas walk. (Yes, really!) There's a really good small zoo on the Downs, too. It's called Drusillas Park and there are meerkats, lemurs, monkeys, penguins and more. It's really wild!

Meerkats at Drusillas Park near Eastbourne

But what I like best about Eastbourne is the seafront. There's nowhere quite like it in the whole wide world. You can laze on the beach, but if you want to get busy you've come to the right place!

Let me take you on a tour of the seafront …

The beach at Eastbourne

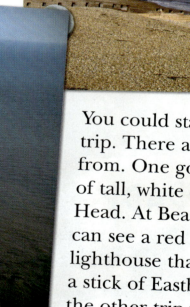

Beachy Head lighthouse

You could start with a boat trip. There are two to choose from. One goes out past a line of tall, white cliffs to Beachy Head. At Beachy Head you can see a red and white lighthouse that looks a bit like a stick of Eastbourne rock! On the other trip you can go rushing across the waves in a speedboat – you'll have lots of thrills and a *splashing* time!

Next, check out Fort Fun. It has some really good rides. The Runaway Train speeds round tight bends. The Bat Ride zooms up to the sky.

Big screams on The Runaway Train

The scary Bat Ride

Along the seafront you'll find the Wish Tower Puppet Museum. It has puppets from all over the world. Many of them have been on TV and in films. It's a cool place, but don't stay too long – there are too many other things to do!

Puppet maker Mel Myland at his puppet museum

For example, you could jump on the Dotto Train and ride beside the sea.

The famous Eastbourne Dotto Train

Then you could end a busy day with a trip to the marina. There, you can look at the boats and enjoy a big ice cream.

Having fun at Eastbourne Marina

Everyone knows that a day trip to Eastbourne is fun. But being here all year round is a dream come true. How can anywhere else even come close?

I'm sure you agree with me by now: Eastbourne is simply the best. Wouldn't you love to live here, too?

Yours by the seaside,

Best Sports Star: David Beckham

Dear Readers,

I want you to know who I think is the best sports star. There's no doubt about it, David Beckham is simply the best sports star in the whole world.

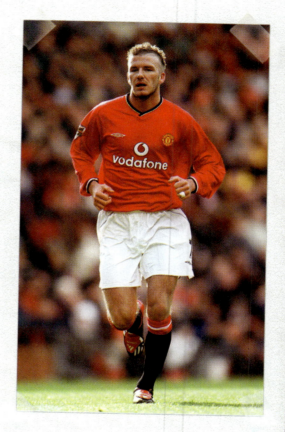

It takes skill, hard work and a little bit of magic to make it to the very top. The truth is, David has all those things and more. All sports stars start out with the same dream; they want to be the best. But experts agree that there's only one David Beckham – and he *is* the best!

Let me tell you a bit about him to prove that's true.

David was born in London in 1975. He grew up near top clubs like Spurs and Arsenal, but he didn't want to play for them. He had his heart set on just one team – Manchester United. He was a quiet boy, but he knew he'd make his dream come true one day. And he was right!

When David was eleven, he went on a soccer holiday run by his hero, Bobby Charlton. Bobby used to play for Manchester United and won the World Cup with England, way back in 1966. Becks won the "best skills" award for his age group on this holiday. He was the best even back then.

Some sports stars let fame go to their heads. When they get to the top, they think they don't have to work hard any more. David Beckham is not like that. He runs, chases and works his socks off in every match. That's why he was made captain of the England team.

Other sports stars feel down in the dumps when things go badly. But soccer fans know that Becks will try his best until the last kick of every game. He never gives up. That's why he's a winner!

England captain

David Beckham is the top sports star in the world. How can anyone argue with that? Let's enjoy two pieces of "Becks magic" over again.

The first was when England played Greece. The game was almost over, but England needed one more goal to get to the World

Cup Finals. They won a free kick a long way out from the goal; one last chance for glory.

As David ran up to take the kick, some fans didn't dare to watch. Seconds later, Becks and his fans were jumping for joy. He had scored a dream goal and England were on their way to the World Cup Finals.

When the tournament started in Japan, the team soon found themselves facing a vital match against their arch rivals, Argentina. The atmosphere was electric. Suddenly, the crowd roared. England had won a penalty. Who had the sheer courage to take this vital kick? David Beckham, of course. He stayed ice cool, smashed the ball into the net, and England won 1-0.

The man is magic. That's what makes David Beckham simply the best!

Yours sportingly,

Tony

Beckham celebrates his dream goal

Best Holiday: Orlando Theme Parks

Dear Readers,

Millions of visitors to Florida agree with me, the theme parks of Orlando are simply the best for holiday fun! People, music, noise and non-stop action ... that's Orlando. How could *anyone* not have fun here? After all, we all want the same things on holiday, don't we?

The runaway train on Thunder Mountain

Tourists flood the theme parks all year long. The warm air is filled with shouts and hoots of laughter. You may have to queue to get on the top rides, but most people agree it's worth it. In fact, waiting in line gives you time to relax between the thrills – so that's a very good thing.

Let's take a look at some of the top theme parks in Orlando. They are very well run and each one has a style of its own.

The most famous of all is Walt Disney World which has four theme parks.

The Magic Kingdom is where you'll meet Mickey Mouse and all the Disney cartoon characters. You can ride on a runaway train, or zoom through the sky on a rocket. And don't forget to meet the spooky ghosts in the haunted house! Who could possibly ask for more?

The famous Disney characters

Animal Kingdom has tigers, gorillas and more, while Epcot offers a trip through time and space on Spaceship Earth. Disney-MGM Studios shows you the magic of the movies ... past, present and future.

Everyone loves films so don't miss the studio tour at Universal Studios which gives you a behind-the-scenes look at how movies are made. You'll see some top stunts and get a scare from a shark called Jaws, too. You're sure to have a *snappy* time!

At Islands of Adventure, you can take a trip to Jurassic Park, enjoy some 3-D action with Spider Man and race round a top roller coaster ride with the Incredible Hulk.

Sea World brings you close to whales, dolphins, polar bears and penguins.

There's no doubt about it, the theme parks of Orlando are brilliant fun.

Florida is hot and humid for much of the year, so it's a good idea to plan your days in the theme parks. If you follow my top five tips you'll be sure to have a holiday of a lifetime:

⭐ Go to the theme parks early and enjoy the best rides first.

⭐ Wear comfortable clothes and have lots of soft drinks.

⭐ Take a break from the theme parks in the heat of the day.

⭐ Go back to the theme parks in the evening. You won't have to wait so long for the top rides. There are some super fireworks shows, too!

⭐ Go to the gift shops just before you leave. Why carry heavy bags all day?

Some people say that, after a week in Orlando's theme parks, they need to go home for a rest – they must be joking!

The millions of fans of Florida theme parks can't be wrong: Orlando is a holiday dream come true. If it's true for them, then it will be true for you, too. I know you'll agree with me that Orlando is simply the best for holiday fun!

Have.a nice day!

Yours dreaming-of-the-sun,

Tony

Best Pop Band: The Beatles

Dear Readers,

I've told you about the best in sport, now let me tell you about the best in music. They sang *All You Need Is Love*, but when it comes to music, all you need is the magical sound of The Beatles. Most music critics agree that they are simply the best band ever!

The Beatles had their first hit with *Love Me Do* in 1962. Their last album, *Let It Be*, came out in 1970. Their music may be over 30 years old now, but it still sounds fresh and exciting. Doesn't that prove they're simply the best?

John Lennon

Paul McCartney

Lots of top bands play good music, but only one can be the best of all time. I bet that you are saying, "Okay, so why pick The Beatles?"

Let's ask ourselves some questions … and the answer will be clear!

Were The Beatles good singers?

Answer: yes. John Lennon and Paul McCartney sang love songs in warm, tender voices. They also roared rock songs with real power. George Harrison had a gentle voice and Ringo was unique! When it came to harmony, The Beatles had a sound all of their own. It makes perfect sense to say that this alone makes them the greatest.

George Harrison

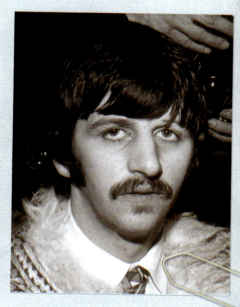

Ringo Starr

Were they good musicians?

Great! John played rhythm guitar and Paul was on bass. George added lead guitar and Ringo played drums. They could all *really play* their instruments. How many other groups can honestly say that?

The Beatles in 1963

Did The Beatles do good live shows?

Of course! When The Beatles were on stage, the fans went wild. The screams were enough to scare a vampire … or even his mummy!

Beatlemania!

The Beatles learnt how to play live long before they became famous. They did lots of all-night shows in the German town of Hamburg. Back home in Liverpool, they worked in a club called The Cavern. So, when their big chance came, they were ready to rock the world!

Do we need to ask any more questions?

Probably not – The Beatles are the best band ever. I know I've proved that already, but we'll carry on just for fun.

Did The Beatles write their own songs?

Yes, hundreds of them. George Harrison wrote classic songs like *Something*, but John Lennon and Paul McCartney wrote many more. They started as schoolboys in Liverpool and the houses where they wrote their first songs are famous now.

John Lennon's childhood home

Paul McCartney's childhood home

Strawberry Field children's home, Liverpool

The Beatles never forgot their home town. Paul wrote about a road called *Penny Lane*; John wrote about a children's home in *Strawberry Fields Forever*. It's a fact: Beatles songs will live forever.

Okay, now let me ask *you* a question.

How many of today's bands will still be played on the radio in 40 years' time?

Surely the answer has to be none, doesn't it?

Experts tell us that a Beatles song is playing somewhere in the world, every minute of every day. From New York to Tokyo and Sydney to London, fans of the Fab Four (and I know that means you) all say the same: The Beatles are simply the best band ever!

I'm going to stop now and play some Beatles music. I wish you could join me!

Yours in-a-Fab-Four-mood,

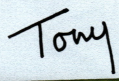

Best Artist: Vincent van Gogh

Dear Readers,

The world has seen many great painters. But for me, and for millions of others, Vincent van Gogh is simply the best. Are artists usually known by their first name alone? No! But just say "Vincent" to people and they will instantly know who you mean.

All the books are right when they say that Vincent is the most famous artist of all time. It stands to reason that if he is the most famous, then he must naturally be the best. I think it's wrong to judge how good a painting is by the price it is sold for, but if Vincent is judged in this way, he naturally passes the test. His paintings are the most expensive in history. Need I say more?

Vincent is world famous now, but the art critics of his day branded him a failure. He produced over 1000 paintings in his lifetime and sold only one. Through all these hard times, Vincent's dedication to his work never faded. How many other artists can really say the same?

Let's remind ourselves of his artistic genius ...

Vincent was born 150 years ago in Holland. In his early life, he drifted from one job to another until he became a painter in 1880, at the age of 27. Over the next ten years he produced a wonderful body of work.

In 1886 he moved to Paris, where he lived for two years with his brother, Theo. Theo was an art dealer and introduced him to a new wave of artists called the Impressionists. Vincent adopted their use of bright colours.

This helped him to develop a style all of his own. No other artist painted quite like Vincent. He was unique and, of course, it was being different that has made him the best.

In 1888 Vincent moved to Provence, in the south of France. He loved the clear blue skies and golden yellows of the sunflowers and harvest fields. Through the long hot summer, Vincent worked at a furious pace.

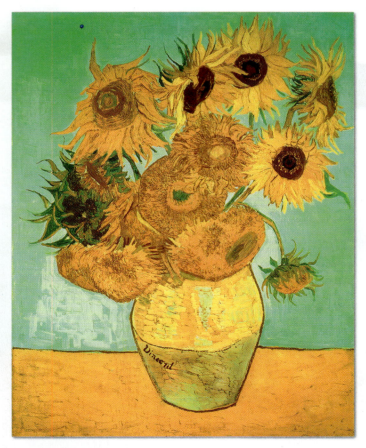

Sunflowers

Road with Cypresses

He even painted at night, with candles on his hat. People said he was mad but Vincent's night paintings are superb. They include two of my favourites, *Café At Night* and *Road with Cypresses*. Could anyone look at these paintings and not be moved?

Vincent burned with the fire of genius in Provence, but he paid the price. Just before Christmas 1888, worn out and lonely, he cut off part of his ear. It was the beginning of the end for this brilliant, tormented man.

A self protrait of Vincent with his bandaged ear

How could anyone not agree that no artist ever suffered like Vincent?

On 27th July 1890, Vincent shot himself in the chest in a wheat field near Paris. He died two days later with Theo, his loyal brother, at his side. Theo died six months later of a broken heart.

Fans leave yellow flowers as a tribute to Vincent van Gogh

The world has seen many great painters, but none like Vincent van Gogh. Everyone in the world loves his paintings and is moved by the story of this tragic man. Undoubtedly, Vincent is simply the best.

Yours with-thoughts-of-Provence,

Tony

Best Way to Travel: Steam Trains

Dear Readers,

Taking a journey on a steam locomotive is like stepping back in time. It's simply the best!

I've visited steam railways all over the UK. In truth, none of them went very far, but I certainly travelled in style. And when you set out on a journey, that's what really counts, don't you think?

Steam locomotives are the stars of the travel world. I love those old movies, where a steam train pulls into a station at night. There is a sudden rush of yellow light from the long line of railway carriages. Steam covers the platform. Someone is waiting for a long-lost friend, but they are nowhere to be seen. As the train gets ready to leave again, it builds a steady rhythm, like the heart of a huge dragon about to breathe fire. Tension rises, then through the steam the long-lost friend appears …

You don't get that sort of drama on a bus to the town centre!

But what about *modern trains*, or boats and planes? Some people would have you believe that they are all a nightmare, but you know that I'll be fair in what I say, don't you?

Modern trains are often dirty, cramped, crowded and full of people with mobiles saying pathetic things like "*I'm on the train*" in really loud voices. What *is* the point of using modern trains if you are a nervous wreck by the time you arrive at your destination?

Having a miserable time!

Look at cars: stress and hassle on four wheels. Everywhere you go these days, it's the same: thick traffic jams and frustrated drivers. Talk about the road to hell! I can't think of one good thing to say about cars, can you?

The traffic comes to a standstill!

Boats are even worse. I went on a boat trip once and it made me sick. Obviously, there's no reason to try that again!

I admit that flying can be fun, but only if you can afford the best seats. However, most of us can't. We have to put up with cramped seats, crowded aisles, second-rate food and crying babies. Who says flying is the best way to travel? Could any sensible person possibly argue with this?

So, we inevitably come back to the grace and style of those superb steam locomotives. Picture yourself in a restaurant carriage, with soft lamps and white tablecloths, eating a meal that makes your mouth water. The train whistle blows as open countryside slips past outside the window. You're not really going anywhere, but that is not the point.

You're travelling on a classic steam train … and it's simply the best!

Yours wishing-that's-where-we-were-right-now,

Tony

A Final Letter from the Author

Dear Readers,

In this book I have written some letters to try and persuade you as to the best place to live, the best holiday and so on. Have I managed to persuade you to agree with me? Have you come round to my point of view?

Perhaps you can persuade me that I'm wrong and you are right. Why not write to me at this address to tell me why *your* choices are simply the best:

Tony Norman
c/o Pelican Guided Reading and Writing
Schools Division
Pearson Education
Edinburgh Gate
Harlow
Essex
CM20 2JE

Looking forward to hearing from you.

Tony